BEFORE YOU BEGIN . . .

This is a book to help you imagine and dream. *Make Beliefs* encourages you to view your world differently, to see new possibilities, and make new choices. All you have to do is use your imagination and your heart to respond to this book's questions.

Each of us is capable of being more than we are if we can catch our breath for a while, lose some of our fears, and try to imagine what things would be like if such and such would happen. That is what *Make Beliefs* tries to do.

By trying to answer this book's "make beliefs" you may come to understand that each of us has the power to realize there is more than one way to see life, that there are many possibilities we can explore through our imagination.

In thinking up these "make beliefs" I wanted to write a book of happiness and hope, to help myself and all of us when we feel there is nothing there. I wanted to create something beautiful to overcome the darkness; each of us holds the key to our own peace if we use our imaginations and make believe sometimes.

You can write, draw, and color your responses to the "make beliefs" throughout the book, and jot down the date you did so in the square boxes provided on each page. You will also find some blank pages to encourage you to write or draw your thoughts, your musings, your dreams, your own doodles—or even your own make-beliefs. Please fill in with crayon or paint the lovely funny drawings to bring color to this book and to your life.

Make Beliefs is a play book for you to explore the foolishness and beauty within your heart and imagination, to find comfort in yourself through your imagination. This is a book of love and affirmation. A book that only you can complete.

So, enjoy. Play.

—BZ

Everything is possible
---when you imagine.

This book of make-beliefs belongs to

S. Hinzeler

Also by Bill Zimmerman

How to Tape Instant Oral Biographies

MAKE BELIEFS

A way to fool around and explore new possibilities

Bill Zimmerman

(You can write,

draw,

and color *them)*

Drawings by Tom Bloom

BANTAM BOOKS
New York Toronto London Sydney Auckland

For my sister, Cynthia, and my brother, Larry
To make you smile

Translations by Teodorina Bello de Zimmerman.
Special thanks to Teresa Berasi and Arthur Hamparian

MAKE BELIEFS
A Bantam Book/published by arrangement with the author

PRINTING HISTORY
Guarionex Press Ltd edition published 1987
Bantam edition / September 1992

Library of Congress Cataloging-in-Publication Data

Zimmerman, William, 1941–
Make beliefs / Bill Zimmerman.
p.   cm.
ISBN 0-553-37004-9
1. Imagination—Problems, exercises, etc.   2. Creative ability—
Problems, exercises, etc.   3. Self-actualization (Psychology)—
Problems, exercises, etc.   I. Title.
BF408.Z55   1992
153.3—dc20   92-7417
                                                       CIP

Published simultaneously in the United States and Canada

Bantam Books are published by Bantam Books, a division of Bantam
Doubleday Dell Publishing Group, Inc. Its trademark, consisting of the
words "Bantam Books" and the portrayal of a rooster, is Registered in
U.S. Patent and Trademark Office and in other countries. Marca Regis-
trada. Bantam Books, 666 Fifth Avenue, New York, New York 10103.

PRINTED IN THE UNITED STATES OF AMERICA

BVG   0 9 8 7 6 5 4 3 2 1

How You Can Use This Book

I originally wrote *Make Beliefs* for middle-aged children like me. But I soon found that the book, once published, took on its own life. Over the years, I've received letters from a wide range of users—from teachers and children in elementary schools; to teenagers and college students; to young adults looking for fun and a way to play; to business executives seeking a resource to help them relax and become more creative; to people in senior citizen centers and nursing homes wanting help in recapturing their imaginations.

Our best educators and parents understand that playing is learning. Many graduate schools use this book to teach young teachers how to spur creativity and imagination in the classroom. In turn, educators use *Make Beliefs* to encourage youngsters to practice language, reading, and creative skills. Many teachers try the individual "make beliefs" as subjects for essays, poems, and plays. Some have even blown up the individual pages and asked each student in a class to make his or her contribution. Others have simply taken the questions from a page and encouraged children to make their own drawings or essays.

The best "make beliefs" are those that readers create for themselves. *Make Beliefs* helps us rely on our imaginations to get us through life's tough times instead of depending on any single book or person or philosophy. The underlying belief of *Make Beliefs* is: There is no greater force in life than the power of the imagination to free us from our immediate problems and to spur our energies to find solutions to our befuddlements.

Many activity directors at social agencies that work with abused or disabled children or adults with special needs, or with elderly people who have withdrawn, have used the book's magical, whimsical drawings and suppositions as a way to draw clients out of their silences and to give voice to their feelings and imagination. Nothing is better than the smell of a fresh box of crayons, newly sharpened pencils, or a jar of paint to stir our senses and produce creative feelings. The drawings provoke reader reactions. As they create their own responses, readers get a better sense of themselves.

For those who teach young and old how to read and learn English as a second language, *Make Beliefs* has become an invaluable tool for helping people try their new language skills in a nonthreatening manner. Many of the pages in this new Bantam edition, in fact, have English-Spanish translations, reflecting peoples' desire to learn more than one language—and to have fun.

In the workplace, where there is so much emphasis today on creativity, *Make Beliefs*, along with Magic Markers, has often been used to trigger brainstorms in harried, tired executives. Many managers pack the book in their briefcases to take to meetings. Think what would happen at your next Monday morning meeting if the conference table or walls were papered with brown drawing paper, and every executive was given a box of crayons along with a yellow pad, and you became children again for an hour! What a better world we'd have. Yes?

In using this new, expanded edition of *Make Beliefs* as an educational resource, you will find that its drawings depict a diverse universe of people of all colors, cultures, ages, and needs. Some people use wheelchairs, crutches, and Seeing Eye dogs. Not all people look the same, and Tom Bloom, Bantam, and I are all trying in this book to reflect the richness of different peoples in our world.

For those of you who are parents, grandparents, aunts and uncles, or big brothers and sisters, why not sit down with the children in your life one night or Sunday morning and do a "make belief" together? It will give you a unique insight into how your minds and spirits work. If your child is too young to read the questions on the page, you can read them aloud and ask the child to color in or dictate a response that you can write for them. This will reinforce the value of their creative voice.

Above all, in having fun with *Make Beliefs*, please remember to convey to a child, and to yourself, the important message that there is no single "right" answer to each "make belief"—only ones that come from the heart.

—BZ

MAKE BELIEVE YOU WERE DANCING ON THE MOON

WHAT KIND OF MUSIC WOULD YOU WANT?

DATE

WHICH
ONE
WOULD
YOU
LIKE?

A PAGE FOR DISCOVERY

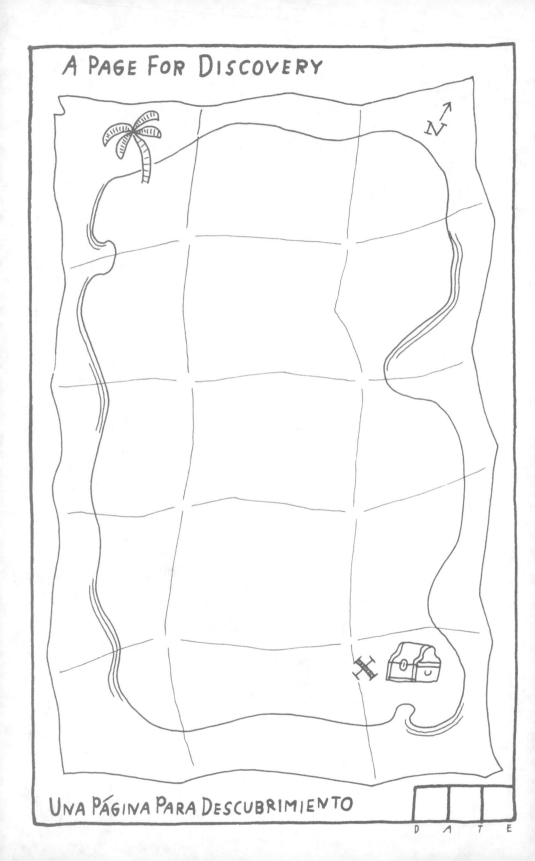

UNA PÁGINA PARA DESCUBRIMIENTO

MAKE BELIEVE

RAINBOWS WERE HANDED TO YOU

WHAT
WOULD YOU DO
WITH THEM AND HOW WOULD THEY FEEL?

A HAPPY PAGE

UNA PÁGINA ALEGRE

DATE

DATE

YOUR LIFE....HOW WOULD YOU PICTURE YOUR PAST?

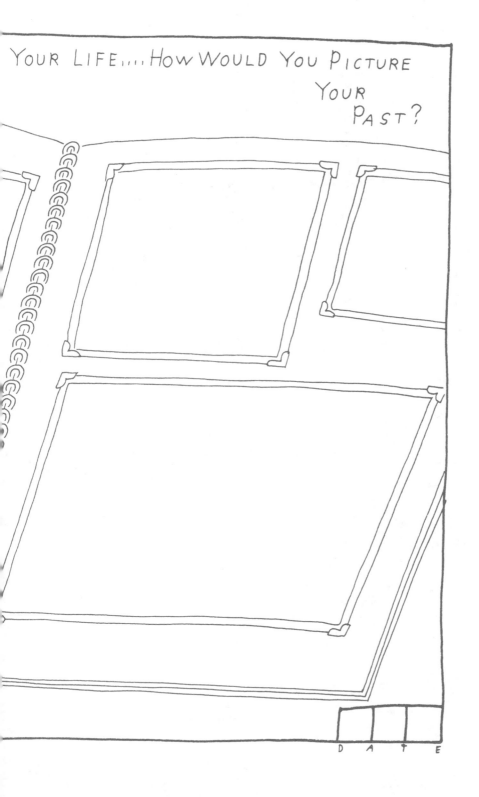

DATE

WHERE WOULD YOUR
TRAVELS TAKE YOU?

...NA ALFOMBRA MÁGICA QUE
VOLABA, ¿POR DÓNDE
VIAJARÍA?

A PAGE FOR BEING CURIOUS

UNA
PÁGINA
PARA
CURIOSIDAD

A BLANK PAGE

UNA PÁGINA EN BLANCO

MAKE BELIEVE
YOU CREATED
  YOUR OWN
  SWEET BLESSING
FOR
SOMEONE
YOU
LOVE

WHAT WOULD IT BE ?

DATE

MAKE BELIEVE YOU LEFT
A MESSAGE FOR
SOMEONE
YOU LOVE DEEPLY

IMAGÍNESE
QUE DEJÓ UN MENSAJE PARA ALQUIEN
QUE ES EL AMOR DE SU VIDA.
QUÉ DIRÍA?

MAKE BELIEVE ONCE A YEAR YOU COULD TRANSFORM YOURSELF INTO A DIFFERENT CREATURE

WHAT WOULD YOU BECOME?

DATE

WHAT WOULD YOU GIVE?

....AND WHY?

DATE

ANOTHER BLANK PAGE

OTRA PÁGINA EN BLANCO

D   A   T   E

MAKE BELIEVE You Could Play Again With An Old, Old Friend

Who Would You Pick To Play With?

WHAT WOULD YOU PLAY?

DATE

A LINED PAGE

UNA PÁGINA RAYADA

A PAGE TO UNWIND

UNA PÁGINA PARA DESENROLLARSE

DATE

DATE

A SAFE PLACE FOR DREAMS

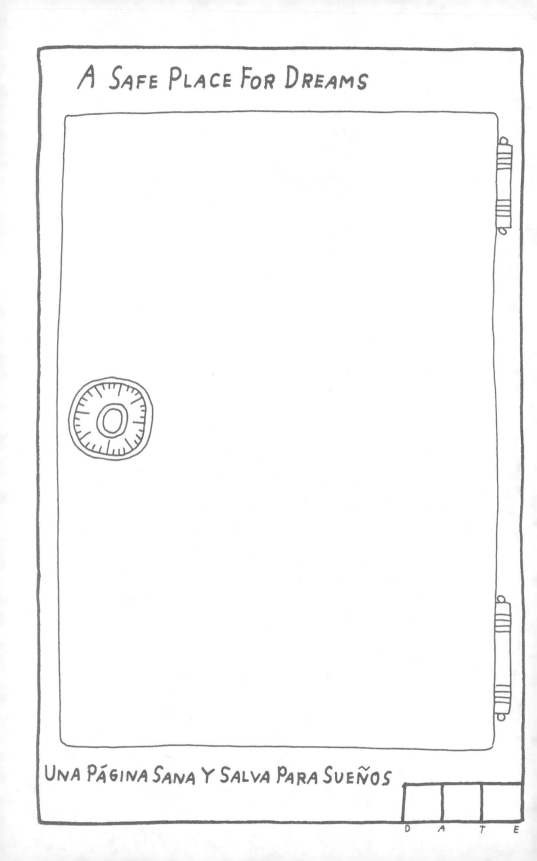

UNA PÁGINA SANA Y SALVA PARA SUEÑOS

D A T E

HOW WOULD YOU DEPICT IT ?

DATE

A PAGE FOR PAUSE

UNA PÁGINA PARA DETENERSE

DATE

A HARBOR FOR LONGINGS

UN PUERTO PARA NOSTAGLIA

DATE

MAKE BELIEVE
YOU WERE TO
LEAVE THE
FLAME
OF YOUR LIFE
TO
SOMEONE...

WHO

IS THAT SOMEONE?

LA PÁGINA NO ESTA EN BLANCO

THIS IS NOT A BLANK PAGE

DATE

WOULD YOU GO WITH YOUR LIFE?

IMAGÍNESE
QUE TUVIERA ALAS PARA VOLAR,
¿A DÓNDE IRÍA CON
SU VIDA?

DATE

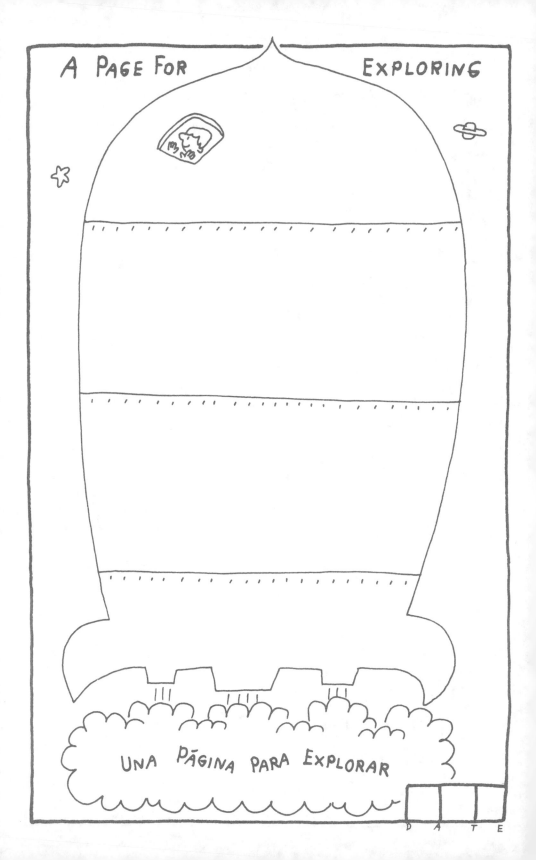

MAKE BELIEVE YOU COULD FIND A SWEET VOICE TO SING WITH

WHEN WOULD YOU USE IT AND HOW WOULD THE SONG GO?

D A T E

A Page For Mistakes

Una Página Para Errores

DATE

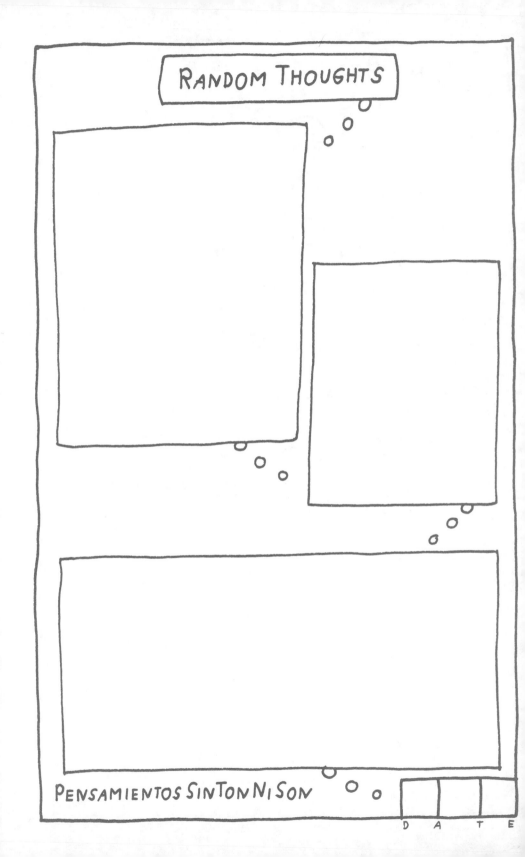

RANDOM THOUGHTS

PENSAMIENTOS SINTON NISON

DATE

DATE

A Sweet Page

UNA PÁGINA DULCE

A PLACE FOR SMILES

UN SITIO PARA SONRISAS

ROOM FOR A JOKE

ESPACIO
PARA UN
CHISTE

DATE

MAKE BELIEVE THAT YOUR MEAL CONSISTED ONLY OF FLOWERS.... WHAT WOULD BE FOR DINNER?

Menu

✿ APPETIZERS ✿

_____
_____
_____
_____

✿ ✿ ENTREE ✿ ✿

_____
_____
_____

✿ SOUP ✿   ✿ SALAD ✿

_____   _____
_____   _____
_____   _____

✿ DESSERT ✿

_____
_____
_____

Thanks

DATE

MAKE BELIEVE THAT WEARING A MASK COULD TRANSFORM YOU INTO THE PERSON YOU THOUGHT YOU WANTED TO BE. HOW WOULD YOU DIFFER FROM THE WAY YOU ARE NOW?

A SPECIAL PLACE FOR PASSIONS

UN ESPACIO ESPECIAL PARA PASIONES

DATE

A NEST FOR A REST

UN NIDO PARA DESCANZO

DATE

MAKE BELIEVE SOMEONE GAVE YOU A GOLDEN TREASURE BOX. WHAT WOULD YOU PLACE IN IT?

OR HOPE TO FIND INSIDE?

DATE

A Relief Page

Una Página Para Relajo

DATE

MAKE BELIEVE
YOU COULD ASK A BIRD
TO DELIVER A
SPECIAL MESSAGE....

WHAT
WOULD IT
SAY
AND TO
WHOM
WOULD YOU
SEND IT?

» SPECIAL MESSAGE «

DATE

MAKE BELIEVE YOU HAD A CHANCE
TO WALK DOWN
A SECRET PATH
TO SOMETHING
WONDERFUL

WHAT WOULD YOU HOPE TO DISCOVER
AT THE END?

_____
_____
_____
_____
_____
_____
_____
_____
_____
_____
_____
_____
_____

MAKE BELIEVE
YOU COULD
TELL A
LOVE STORY
HOW WOULD IT GO?

DATE

MUSINGS

PENSATIVOS

DATE

MAKE BELIEVE IT RAINED BUTTERFLIES

WHAT DO YOU THINK

THE PUDDLES WOULD LOOK LIKE?

DATE

MAKE BELIEVE YOU COULD TRAVEL TO A MYSTERIOUS LAND

WHAT STRANGE THINGS WOULD YOU FIND THERE?

HOW WOULD IT FEEL TO WALK ON COLOR AND AIR?

AFTER THOUGHTS

PENSAMIENTOS MUCHO DESPUÉS

D A T E

A PLACE FOR HOPES

UN ESPACIO PARA ESPERANZAS

DATE

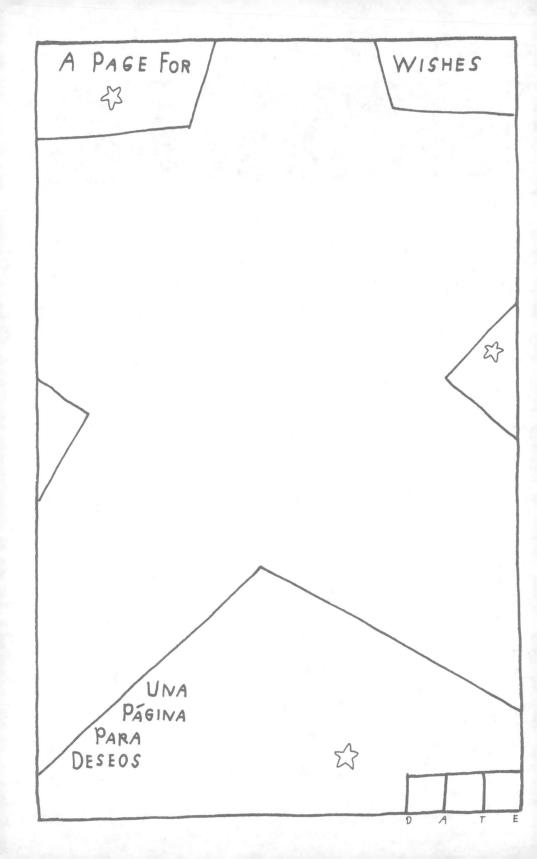

A PAGE FOR   WISHES

UNA
PÁGINA
PARA
DESEOS

DATE

ENDNOTE:

Dear reader,
You may find in trying to answer some of these "make-beliefs"
that you do, indeed, have the power to make some of them
come true.

BILL ZIMMERMAN, the creator of *Make Beliefs*, has been a questioner and dreamer all his life. A prize-winning editor for more than twenty-five years, Zimmerman is special projects editor for *Newsday*, one of the nation's largest tabloid newspapers, where he edits a Student Briefing Page on the News. He also is author of *How to Tape Instant Oral Biographies*, a family oral history guide; *Lifelines: A Book of Hope*, which offers comforting thoughts, and *A Book of Questions to Keep Thoughts and Feelings*, a new form of diary/journal. Zimmerman, who first published *Make Beliefs* from his kitchen-table press, Guarionex Press, believes in the power of the imagination and human spirit to overcome life's problems. "Dreaming is breathing," he says.

TOM BLOOM LIVES AND DRAWS IN A WORLD OF DREAMS, BOTH THE DAY AND NIGHT-TIME VARIETY. HIS IMMEDIATE WORLD INCLUDES THE PLANET EARTH, WHERE HE LIVES WITH HIS WIFE AND KIDS, THE NEW YORK TIMES, THE NEW YORKER (YES.), FORTUNE MAGAZINE, NEW YORK WOMAN, WOMANS DAY, AND NEWSDAY WHERE HIS WORK OFTEN APPEARS, AS IF BY MAGIC.

CREATE YOUR OWN "MAKE BELIEF" QUESTION FOR PUBLICATION OR WIN A COPY OF ONE OF MY BOOKS FOR FREE!*

Dear Reader,

In using this book, you may have begun to think of your own magical "Make Belief" questions. If you would like to share them with me, please send them with your name, age, address, and phone number to the address below. Bantam and I will include the most imaginative and heart-felt "Make Belief" question in a future publication of one of my books. Runners-up will receive a copy of one of my books for free.

Please send your "Make Belief" questions to:

Bill Zimmerman
c/o Bantam Books
Dept. MH
666 Fifth Avenue
New York, New York 10103

Thank you and keep using your imagination—it's your most precious resource.

For official contest rules, see next page.

BANTAM'S
MAKE BELIEFS READER'S CONTEST

OFFICIAL RULES

1. No purchase necessary. To enter, create an original "Make Belief" question and write and/or draw it on an 8½" × 11" sheet of paper with your name, age, address, and phone number printed at the bottom and mail it to: Bill Zimmerman, c/o Bantam Books, Dept. MH, 666 Fifth Avenue, New York, New York 10103. There is no limit to the number of entries that may be submitted, but each entry must be original and each entry must be mailed separately.

2. 1 First Place Prize: Inclusion of the Winner's "Make Belief" question in a future publication of one of Bill Zimmerman's books and 6 free copies of that book. (Approximate retail value: $51.00)

   25 Runner-Up Prizes: A free copy of one of Bill Zimmerman's books. (Approximate retail value: $8.50)

3. The contest begins on August 1, 1992. All entries must be postmarked and received no later than December 1, 1992. Entries will be judged on the basis of their creativity, originality, and sincerity. The winners will be selected by a panel of judges that will include MAKE BELIEFS' author, Bill Zimmerman, and members of Bantam's Editorial and Publisher's departments. In the event there are an insufficient number of entries that meet the standards established by the judges, Bantam reserves the right not to award the prizes. The judges' decision will be final. Winners will be notified by mail on or about December 30, 1992, and will have 30 days from the date of notification to accept the prize award or an alternative winner will be chosen. Bantam is not responsible for lost, misdirected, or incomplete entries. The odds of winning are dependent on the number of entries received. All "Make Belief" questions become the property of Bantam Books and none will be returned. All "Make Belief" questions entered must be the original creation of the entrant and the entrant's sole and exclusive property.

4. The First Place Winner may be required to execute an Affidavit of Eligibility and Promotional Release supplied by Bantam.

5. Entering the contest constitutes permission for use of the winner's name, age, address, likeness, and contest entry for publicity and promotional purposes with no additional compensation.

6. The contest is open to residents of the U.S.A. and Canada, excluding the province of Quebec. Void where prohibited or restricted by law. Employees of Bantam Books, Bantam Doubleday Dell Publishing Group Inc., their affiliates, subsidiaries, and divisions, and employees' immediate family members are not eligible to enter. Taxes, if any, are the winner's sole responsibility.

7. For a list of winners, send a self-addressed stamped envelope after December 30, 1992 to: Winners, Bantam's MAKE BELIEFS Reader's Contest, Bantam Books, Dept. MH, 666 Fifth Avenue, New York, New York 10103.